D0974375

Sticky Faith Curriculum

FULLER YOUTH INSTITUTE

Can I Ask That?
Volume 2: More Hard Questions about God & Faith

STUDENT GUIDE

A Sticky Faith Curriculum

Copyright © 2015 by Jim Candy, Brad M. Griffin, & Kara Powell

All Rights Reserved

Sticky Faith is a trademark of the Fuller Youth Institute at Fuller Theological Seminary and is registered with the United States Patent and Trademark Office.

Published in the United States of America by
Fuller Youth Institute, 135 N. Oakland Ave., Pasadena, CA, 91182
fulleryouthinstitute.org

ISBN 978-0-9914880-3-2

Unless otherwise noted, all scripture quotations are taken from THE HOLY BIBLE, NEW INTERNATIONAL VERSION®, NIV® Copyright © 1973, 1978, 1984, 2011 by Biblica, Inc.®

All rights reserved. No part of this publication may be reproduced, stored in a retrieval system, or transmitted in any form or by any means—electronic, mechanical, photocopy, recording, or any other—except for those parts intended as distributable handouts or digital resources, without the prior permission of the publisher.

Cover Design: Matthew Schuler
Interior Design: Macy Phenix Davis, Matthew Schuler, Fuller Youth Institute

Copy Editor: Dana Wilkerson

Printed in the United States of America

Sticky Faith Curriculum

STUDENT

CAN I ASK THAT

VOLUME 2

JIM CANDY
BRAD M. GRIFFIN
KARA POWELL

**MORE HARD QUESTIONS
ABOUT GOD & FAITH**

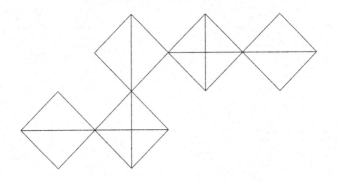

1   *Is it wrong to doubt God?*

2   *Is hell real? How could God send someone there?*

3   *Can I do something so bad God won't forgive me?*

4   *Why do bad things happen to good people?*

5   *Is sex outside marriage wrong?*

6   *Why is it so awkward to talk about Jesus with my friends?*

\/\/ *Ten tips for reading your Bible*

Can I Ask That?

It was the little things that did it.

Not big stuff like doubting the existence of God altogether, but little stuff. Like hanging out with her best friend from Thailand whose family practiced Buddhism. Or her church leaders' lack of response to two huge back-to-back incidents of racial injustice in national news.

It was the little things that led to Kayla's drift from God.

One of those little things was the way her parents responded when she pointed out things in the Bible that didn't make sense or didn't seem very loving. How could God be all-loving and then damn good people to hell for eternity? Can we do anything that God wouldn't forgive? Whenever Kayla raised a question like this, her parents either flipped out or shut her down with their blanket response for everything: "We just have to trust that the Bible is right and not expect it to defend God to us."

At church it was more subtle. Kayla could see her volunteer youth leaders' inconsistencies in the way they were living outside of church and by what they shared on social media.

— — —

She wasn't sure she really knew any people who were living out all the stuff they said they believed. And whenever someone questioned God or a Bible passage in youth group, the high school pastor would respond without really answering the question and then change the subject.

Yeah, lots of little things.

So when Kayla found herself as a junior telling her parents that she didn't want to go to youth group anymore, she couldn't fully explain why. But she knew what she couldn't do: ask questions. For too long and from too many voices, her questions just didn't seem good enough for the church or her parents. Or God.

Or maybe the bigger problem was that God wasn't big enough to handle real questions. Who needs a God like that?

Yes, you can ask

that

Yes, you can ask that.

It's probably not a surprise that many high school and college students deal with intense challenges to their faith. Some of those challenges come from outside, while others are doubts that sneak up from the inside. Maybe you've experienced some of both kinds of struggles yourself.

We've listened to the questions of teenagers like you, and we've written these sessions to openly explore the hot topics you take seriously or have questions about. These sessions will raise *tough questions* about your faith in God. The issues are challenging—so much so that some of the leading scholars in the world don't agree on their answers. The good news about that is you'll get to explore different viewpoints on some of Christianity's most avoided topics.

Most importantly, this study will help you think about what *you believe* in light of scripture and the insights of others. Belief is often something that changes and grows as you do. We hope you'll grow to trust Christ more as you wrestle with the hard questions we'll explore together:

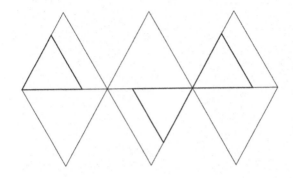

The six sessions tackle the following tough questions:

⊗ *Is it wrong to doubt God?*

⊗ *Is hell real? How could God send someone there?*

⊗ *Can I do something so bad God won't forgive me?*

⊗ *Why do bad things happen to good people?*

⊗ *Is sex outside marriage wrong?*

⊗ *Why is it so awkward to talk about Jesus with my friends?*

What you should know
before you start

Here are a few important keys to help you along the way:

KEY #1:
This is about faith that sticks.

Sticky Faith is an initiative from the Fuller Youth Institute designed to understand and help faith "stick" in teenagers (see stickyfaith.org). In other words, we want to see young people grow in faith in Christ as they grow into adults. We have observed through research that wrestling with doubt—even doubt in God—can be a very healthy process. We hope this study helps you have real conversations with God and each other about difficult topics.

KEY #2: Don't hold back.

ANY questions or doubts you have are welcome. In fact, they are required. Be honest. See what God might do with you—and in you—through this process. God is not biting fingernails, nervous about the tough questions you might ask. God is also not going to be angry or annoyed by doubt. Do not be afraid to use the words, "I don't know" in the face of tough questions. Those words acknowledge that we have a big God. We'll talk about this theme more in the opening session.

KEY #3:
Learn the "context."

To understand what the Bible means, we need to understand *what it meant for the people who wrote and read it "way back then."* Studying the context means discovering who wrote the Bible, to whom they wrote, and why.

For example, imagine a friend of yours is in class and her phone buzzes. Someone texted your friend from a number she doesn't recognize:

I've been secretly wanting to ask you this for a while now ... Prom?

Because she doesn't recognize the number, she doesn't know whether to be excited or angry. The author and that person's intentions are unknown. Is it a friend playing a joke on her from someone else's phone? Is it the guy she dreams about? Was it sent to her accidentally?

Without the *context* of this mystery text message, she doesn't know what it means. The Bible is the same way. We need to know who wrote the passage (when possible), why they wrote it, and for what individual or community it was written. Context is crucial for understanding a passage.

For that reason, the "Notes" part of each session shares a little context for key passages.

> **KEY #4:**
> *Don't study alone.*

These sessions should be studied with other people, not alone. One prayer for you is that you find adults who really care about you and about your faith journey. Some of you may not have someone older who invited you to study this together. If that's you, ask yourself, "Is there any adult I trust who loves Jesus?" Consider asking that person to discuss these sessions with you.

> **KEY #5: Ask God for help.**

This study will probably bring up challenging questions and potentially big breakthroughs for you. Jesus promises the Holy Spirit lives in us to help us make sense of the scriptures. Take God up on this promise, and ask the Holy Spirit to guide you as you begin this adventure!

Session

1 Is it wrong to doubt God?

Terrence's sophomore year was a disaster.

His life was full of challenges that birthed colossal doubts about the existence and goodness of God.

First, there was his friend Ethan. Ethan had struggled for as long as Terrence could remember. Ethan's mom was diagnosed with depression after his dad left two years ago, and Ethan often questioned whether life was worth living. Terrence would never forget the day his friend, Sean, called and told him Ethan had overdosed on pain medication and had died.

Was there something I could have done? Terrence wondered, amid tears.

Then there was Lilly, the girl he had dreamed about since sixth grade. He asked her to the Winter Dance and couldn't believe it when she said yes. Terrence had the big night all planned until he found out Lilly, one of the football team's managers, had hooked up with a junior linebacker on the bus ride to the state playoff game. He felt so betrayed. Why were these things happening?

Is God doing this to me? he wondered.

Terrence had always heard, "God loves you," from people at church, but the reality of his messy life and a loving God weren't matching up. He very nervously told the pastor at his church that he was having doubts about God. Terrence explained all that had happened that year and wondered aloud why God wasn't helping him out. The pastor looked at him with a bit of shock.

"Terrence, the Bible is very clear about doubt," the pastor said. "The book of James says that anyone who doubts is an 'unstable person.' Ask God to help you, because God loves people who believe without questioning."

Terrence suddenly felt ashamed for admitting doubts to the pastor. *I swear I will never do that again,* Terrence promised himself.

The next week, Terrence was reading for a physics project when he ran across an article titled: "'God Particle' Discovery Ignites Debate Over Science and Religion."

The article described a new type of matter discovered in the universe and quoted a professor saying the God Particle "posits a new story of our creation" independent of religious belief.[1] The article seemed to suggest this new discovery made God irrelevant.

Maybe life is all just an accident, Terrence wondered. *I know my life feels like an accident.*

Terrence didn't know what to believe and had no one he trusted to talk to about his doubts.

(questions)

If you were friends with Terrence and knew what he was feeling and thinking, what would you do or say?

What do you think of the pastor's statement, "God loves people who believe without questioning"? What about his approach to Terrence?

What kinds of doubts have you heard other people express about God?

When you question God, which doubt is most common for you? Circle all that apply.

a.   I doubt God exists.

b.   I doubt God is good.

c.   I doubt God is powerful.

d.   I doubt God cares or I think God is angry with me.

e.   I have a different doubt than the ones above.

n *(notes)*

A Nervous God

Are there questions that could make God nervous? Some people believe that God will punish those who doubt. But if God is really all-powerful and has nothing to hide, would God fear human questioning? Why would God be opposed to it?

Intellectual vs. Emotional Doubts

There are different kinds of doubts. Some people doubt God because they intellectually wonder if God exists. They often view science and creation as incompatible and can't mentally consent to belief in God. Others doubt due to an emotional barrier. Perhaps something has happened to them that makes belief in God difficult.

> What are other examples of intellectual and emotional doubts? Which kind of doubt do you see in Terrence?

> Do your own doubts and questions tend toward more emotional or more intellectual issues?

What Does Doubt Do?

Well-known pastor John Ortberg says doubt does important things for our faith journey.

Doubt:

1. makes trust possible

2. adds humility to our faith

3. helps us learn

4. pushes us to seek truth

5. leads to growth[2]

> Which of those five things do you believe is most true? Why?

Does Doubt Make You Unstable?

Terrence's pastor references a verse in James about doubt. He is arguing that doubt is something God frowns on. Take a quick look at James 1:5-8.

If any of you lacks wisdom, you should ask God, who gives generously to all without finding fault, and it will be given to you. But when you ask, you must believe and not doubt, because the one who doubts is like a wave of the sea, blown and tossed by the wind. That person should not expect to receive anything from the Lord. Such a person is double-minded and unstable in all they do.

– James 1:5-8

What do you think James is trying to say about doubt here? What kinds of doubts is he talking about?

Can doubt ever become toxic?

Can certainty about faith ever become toxic?

S   (*scripture*)

Okay, get ready.

You want to see some real doubt in action? Check out the prayer we find in Psalm 88. The Psalms are filled with prayers that question, doubt, and express anger toward God. These are called laments, and over a third of the Psalms in scripture are like this.

Read Psalm 88:1-9, 13-18.

LORD, you are the God who saves me; day and night I cry out to you.

May my prayer come before you; turn your ear to my cry.

I am overwhelmed with troubles and my life draws near to death.

I am counted among those who go down to the pit; I am like one without strength.

I am set apart with the dead, like the slain who lie in the grave, whom you remember no more, who are cut off from your care.

You have put me in the lowest pit, in the darkest depths.

Your wrath lies heavily on me; you have overwhelmed me with all your waves.

You have taken from me my closest friends and have made me repulsive to them. I am confined and cannot escape; my eyes are dim with grief.

But I cry to you for help, LORD; in the morning my prayer comes before you.

Why, LORD, do you reject me and hide your face from me?

From my youth I have suffered and been close to death; I have borne your terrors and am in despair.

Your wrath has swept over me; your terrors have destroyed me.

All day long they surround me like a flood; they have completely engulfed me.

You have taken from me friend and neighbor—darkness is my closest friend.

– Psalm 88:1-9, 13-18

What surprises you about this passage?

Is this an example of emotional or intellectual doubt? Why?

Jesus experienced doubt from lots of sources, including his closest friends, the religious leaders, people he met on his travels, and even his own family. (See John 7:5 for an example of Jesus' brothers expressing doubt.)

He also prayed a psalm of lament from the cross, "My God, my God, why have you forsaken me?" (Psalm 22:1, Matthew 27:46, Mark 15:34)

Read John 20:24-29 for an example from one of his closest followers who struggled to believe in Jesus' resurrection:

Now Thomas (also known as Didymus), one of the Twelve, was not with the disciples when Jesus came. So the other disciples told him, "We have seen the Lord!"

But he said to them, "Unless I see the nail marks in his hands and put my finger where the nails were, and put my hand into his side, I will not believe."

A week later his disciples were in the house again, and Thomas was with them. Though the doors were locked, Jesus came and stood among them and said, "Peace be with you!" Then he said to Thomas, "Put your finger here; see my hands. Reach out your hand and put it into my side. Stop doubting and believe."

Thomas said to him, "My Lord and my God!"

Then Jesus told him, "Because you have seen me, you have believed; blessed are those who have not seen and yet have believed."

– John 20:24-29

What do you notice about how Jesus responds?

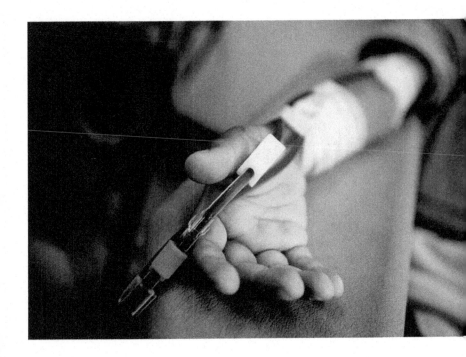

 *(talk)*

Pretend you are with some Christian friends who give their opinions on this topic. Read their comments and write one sentence after each comment that points out a weakness in that person's argument.

DANIA

Doubt shows weakness to people who don't believe in God. If a non-Christian doesn't believe in God and sees Christians doubting, how can we ever expect people to end up believing in Jesus?

JOSH

Doubt is okay, but it should be kept private. My experience with telling others about my doubts isn't good. People end up thinking you aren't really strong in what you believe. It's better to just keep it to yourself.

BRITTA

I think every sermon, book, or conversation about God should be critiqued. My motto is: "Always find the counterargument." My faith is much stronger because I'm constantly using my mind.

MICAH

It's important to be really open about doubt. I like to make sure everyone knows my doubts, so I'm always telling people about them. If people don't respond well, that's their problem.

List a few people you can go to with questions who will take you—and your questions— seriously. What do you hope you will talk about or do together?

Footnotes

1. Chris Lisee, "Higgs Boson: 'God Particle' Discovery Ignites Debate Over Science and Religion," *Huffington Post,* July 14, 2012.

2. John Ortberg, *Faith and Doubt* (Grand Rapids: Zondervan, 2008), 135-149.

Ideas / Notes

Session

2

Is hell real? How could God send someone there?

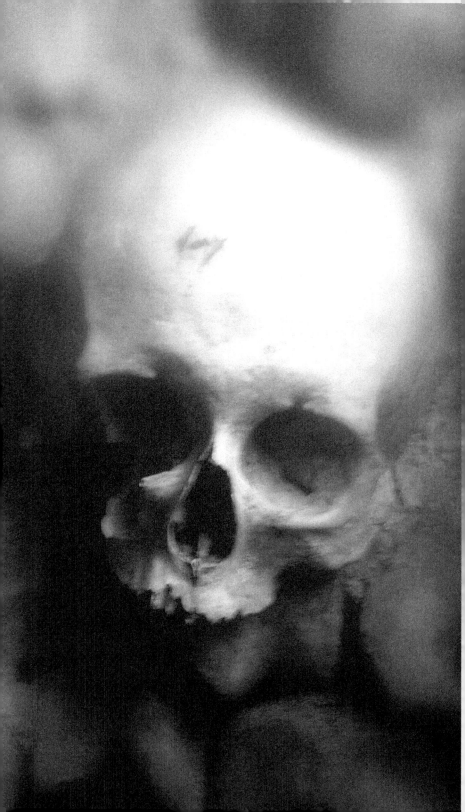

Gina's grandma died on a Thursday morning.

After days of crying and the family arriving into town, Monday afternoon's funeral was wonderful. Gina's grandma was loved. She was outgoing and funny. Her favorite TV show was *Everybody Loves Raymond*, which endeared her to her grandkids. She was tremendously generous in donating her time to help a local homeless shelter.

At the funeral, the pastor spoke about how kind and generous Gina's grandma was and how wonderful it would be to see her again someday with God in heaven.

Gina's family, cousins, aunts, and uncles all went to dinner after the service. Gina didn't know them all that well because they lived so far away, but she knew her Uncle Chad was "very, very,

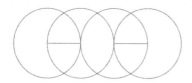

very religious," as Gina's mom would say. Gina got nervous when Chad started asking questions.

"What did you think of the funeral?" Uncle Chad asked Gina and her two sisters.

"It was nice," Gina's older sister Johanna replied, "but sad. I miss my grandma already."

"Do you believe what the pastor said about your grandma going to heaven?" Chad said. "I thought she wasn't a Christian."

It was true. Gina's grandma, while very kind-hearted, made it clear to everyone that she was not a Christian. She didn't believe in God at all. Gina had heard from her mom that a teacher in a Christian school had treated Grandma cruelly when she was a child. It made such an impact on her that she had refused to believe in God's existence ever since.

"I guess I don't really know," Gina said to her uncle, not wanting to get into a debate with him on the day of the funeral.

"Well, I know," Chad replied. "The truth is that people who don't believe in God are going to hell. Your grandma is not going to be in heaven."

Gina's younger sister Bridgette burst into tears.

"Uncle Chad says Grandma is going to hell," she sobbed. Others around the table quickly took notice. It didn't take long before a verbal brawl ensued. Chad's wife even yelled at Chad for being insensitive. Bridgette continued to whimper quietly until her other uncle, Max, whispered to her.

"Your uncle Chad doesn't know what he's talking about, Bridgette," Max said. "Grandma is in heaven now with God. There is no such thing as hell."

Gina loved her church and her student pastor, but nothing they ever talked about had prepared her for this. She started wondering, *Who's right? Is hell real? And if it is, how could a good God send Grandma to hell?*

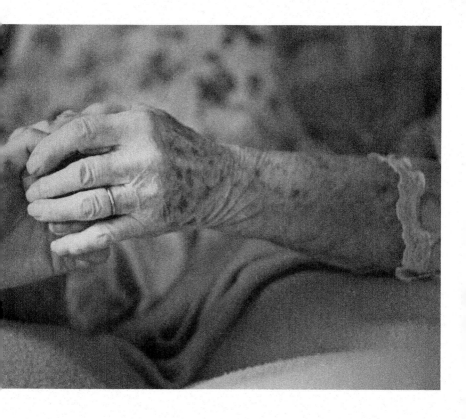

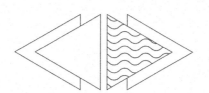

q *(questions)*

What stands out to you the most about this story, and why?

What image comes to your mind when you think of the word "hell"?

What do you think of Uncle Chad's opinions and his approach?

What do you think about what Uncle Max whispered to Bridgette: "Grandma is in heaven now with God. There is no such thing as hell"?

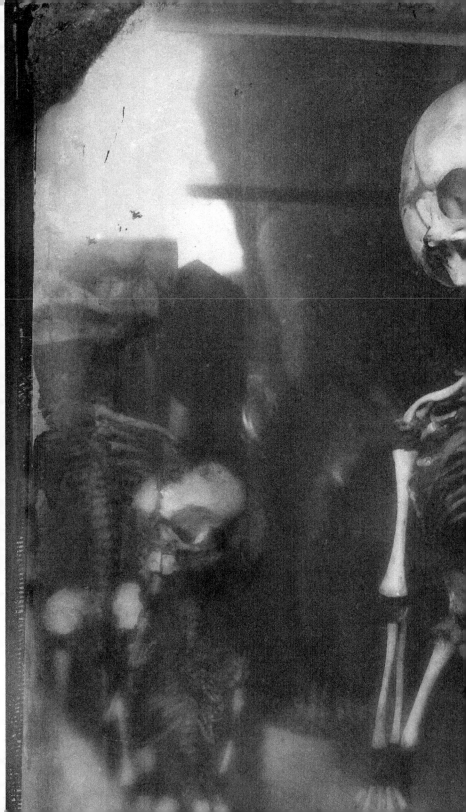

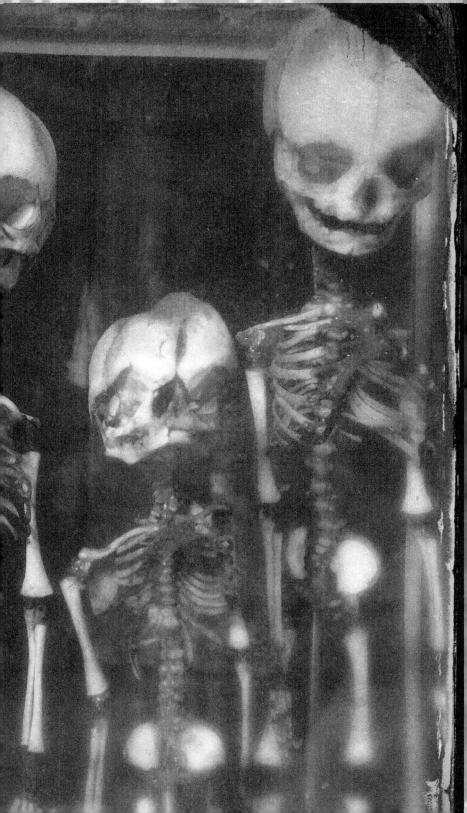

(notes)

A little vocabulary boost:
How does the Bible speak of hell?

Sheol: The Old Testament word "Sheol" was the Hebrew name for what happens after death. While some Bible translations mention "Sheol" specifically in the Old Testament, your Bible translation might use the word "pit" or "grave" instead. Key to our understanding of "Sheol" is realizing that it always indicated both a place and a condition. Hebrew people did not believe in the life of the soul after death, but they did believe in God's power to ultimately rescue the dead someday. Sheol is meant like an interim state for our bodies and souls after death and before that ultimate rescue. Sheol in Greek is "hades," which is why you see that word in the New Testament.

Gehenna: The word more often translated "hell" in the New Testament is "Gehenna." It was the name of an actual valley near the city of Jerusalem where some ancient (and very evil) kings performed child sacrifices to a different god. It became a hated place, and its name was synonymous with somewhere God would judge. When King Josiah banned child sacrifices to other gods, Gehenna became the trash dump of the town. Fires continually burned there as a way of getting rid of the trash, dead animals, and other refuse that were put there.

Jesus made frequent references to Gehenna, using it as an illustration of ultimate judgment. Some of the passages where Jesus talks about or references the fires of Gehenna include Matthew 11:20-24, Matthew 25:41, Mark 9:43-48, Luke 8:31, Luke 10:12-15, Luke 12:5, and John 15:6, just to name a few!

Why do you think Jesus used Gehenna
as imagery for hell?

What questions do these words and images
raise for you about hell and about how
someone might end up there?

Choice: God gave human beings the choice to love Jesus and follow God ... or not. At the center of the concept of heaven is the belief that we can be with God forever. Heaven is the place and time where we are with God without separation. Some Christians understand scripture to say that human beings have the choice either to be one of Jesus' followers or to follow something or someone else. God doesn't force humans to follow Jesus. In this way, God gave us "free will." Others believe that God chooses our eternal destiny and we simply live out what God has already chosen.

Would God be good if you were forced to be with God forever ... against your will?

Universalism: Some believe God will save all people. No one has to experience hell, because God's love—the love that resurrected Christ from eternal punishment—overcame death and hell for all of us. A universalist perspective might look at a passage like John 3:16-17 and assert that Jesus did not come to condemn the world, but to save it.

Annihilationism: Some people believe that God will not send people to a place of eternal punishment but, instead, will annihilate their souls so they cease to exist.

Is hell real? How could God
send someone there?

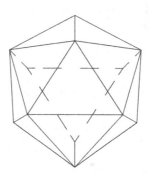

S (scripture)

Read Romans 14:10-13:

*You, then, why do you judge your brother or sister? Or
why do you treat them with contempt? For we will all
stand before God's judgment seat. It is written: "'As surely
as I live,' says the Lord, 'every knee will bow before me;
every tongue will acknowledge God.'" So then, each of us
will give an account of ourselves to God. Therefore let us
stop passing judgment on one another. Instead, make up
your mind not to put any stumbling block or obstacle in
the way of a brother or sister.*

– Romans 14:10-13

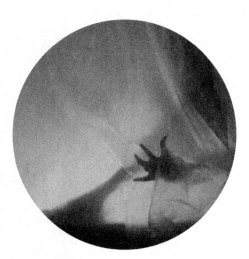

Whose job is it to judge human beings?

Read Matthew 25:31-46:

"When the Son of Man comes in his glory, and all the angels with him, he will sit on his glorious throne. All the nations will be gathered before him, and he will separate the people one from another as a shepherd separates the sheep from the goats. He will put the sheep on his right and the goats on his left.

"Then the King will say to those on his right, 'Come, you who are blessed by my Father; take your inheritance, the kingdom prepared for you since the creation of the world. For I was hungry and you gave me something to eat, I was thirsty and you gave me something to drink, I was a stranger and you invited me in, I needed clothes and you clothed me, I was sick and you looked after me, I was in prison and you came to visit me.'

"Then the righteous will answer him, 'Lord, when did we see you hungry and feed you, or thirsty and give you something to drink? When did we see you a stranger and invite you in, or needing clothes and clothe you? When did we see you sick or in prison and go to visit you?'

"The King will reply, 'Truly I tell you, whatever you did for one of the least of these brothers and sisters of mine, you did for me.'

"Then he will say to those on his left, 'Depart from me, you who are cursed, into the eternal fire prepared for the devil and his angels. For I was hungry and you gave me nothing to eat, I was thirsty and you gave me nothing to drink, I was a stranger and you did not invite me in, I needed clothes and you did not clothe me, I was sick and in prison and you did not look after me.'

"They also will answer, 'Lord, when did we see you hungry or thirsty or a stranger or needing clothes or sick or in prison, and did not help you?'

"He will reply, 'Truly I tell you, whatever you did not do for one of the least of these, you did not do for me.'

"Then they will go away to eternal punishment, but the righteous to eternal life."

– Matthew 25:31-46

Is hell real? How could God send someone there?

In your own words, what is Jesus saying here?

How does this teaching line up with Paul's teaching that we are saved by grace, not by works, so that no one can boast (see Ephesians 2:8-9)?

How do these passages help us to better understand judgment and life after death?

(*talk*)

Pretend you are with some friends who are giving their opinions on this topic. Read their comments and follow the directions below.

ZACH

Hell is not a real place, but a figurative illustration Jesus used. God wouldn't really send people to hell. It was Jesus' way of describing how devastating life is apart from God.

JILL

I was always taught that if I didn't pray a certain prayer and get baptized, I would go to hell. When I was six, my mom helped me pray the right prayer to avoid hell, and then I got baptized at church. I'm all set.

ARIANA

My church is just the opposite. We do infant baptism, and we say faith is from God, not something we do on our own. I don't think I have to "choose" Jesus; he chose me already.

XANDER

Everyone goes to heaven. Hell is just kind of a "threat" to help us behave better. My parents always used to threaten me with punishments so I'd do what they wanted me to do, but then they never actually followed through. Hell is the same idea.

LIZI

I think hell is a real place that people go to if they choose to live a life of not following Jesus. God wouldn't force someone to be in heaven if they didn't want to be there. That doesn't sound like a good God. Jesus seemed to think hell was a real place, which means I do too.

Write a 1 next to the person you most agree with, and then a 2, 3, 4, and finally a 5 for the person you most disagree with. Why did you rank the statements the way you did? Share with others in your group which statement you most agreed with, and why.

What other questions does this study raise for you?

Ideas / Notes

Session

3

Can I do something so bad God won't forgive me?

Ryan showed up

to a church middle school program called Fusion in seventh grade. His friend Lars had invited him. Ryan liked the games, the cool and funny leaders, and a girl named Lorna. For about a year, he never missed a meeting and became well loved.

After Christmas break his eighth grade year, April, the youth pastor, noticed Ryan had not attended Fusion three weeks in a row. She asked one of her volunteers, Thomas, to call Ryan to let him know they missed him. For three weeks, Thomas tried to get in touch with Ryan, but Ryan never returned his messages.

"What happened to Ryan?" April asked Lars one night. "We miss him. Is everything okay?"

"Um, yeah ... about that," Lars said. "I don't think we'll be seeing Ryan anymore."

"Why not?" April asked, disappointed.

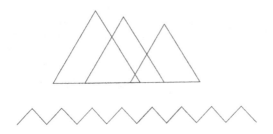

Lars told April what happened over Christmas break. Ryan went to a big New Year's Eve party at a friend's house. He met a group of eighth graders from another school who brought marijuana to the party. Ryan tried it.

"He thinks he's so bad that he shouldn't be at church anymore," Lars said. "I've tried to convince him to come back, but he won't."

April and Thomas kept reaching out to Ryan, but he wouldn't respond. Eventually they gave up.

Meanwhile, Ryan had been feeling guilty. *I know God doesn't want me to be doing this,* he thought. He flipped open his Bible to 1 John 3:9 and read: "No one who is born of God will continue to sin, because God's seed remains in them; they cannot go on sinning, because they have been born of God."

I must not be born of God, Ryan thought. *I decided to follow Jesus last year, and it says I won't sin if I'm from God.*

Ryan felt defeated, and his life began to change drastically after that. He started hanging out with the "potheads," flunked two classes his freshman year, got suspended for punching another student his sophomore year, and started sleeping around with girls his junior year.

His dad, a business exec who was rarely home, threatened to send Ryan to a special school in another part of the state. Ryan tried to apologize and begged to stay.

"If you are really sorry," Ryan's dad said, "you'll stop acting so stupid."

Late in his junior year, Ryan was at a convenience store trying to buy cigarettes after school.

"Ryan? Is that you?"

Ryan recognized the voice and turned. It was April. Ryan felt panic come over him. *What will she say?* he wondered.

"I can't believe it's you!" April said with a smile.

Ryan was surprised. He could tell April was genuinely excited to see him. "It's been years. I've missed you!"

Ryan shifted his gaze. It was hard for him to look her directly in the eye. "Yeah," he said, "I've been a little busy and got sidetracked, I guess."

April decided to take a chance since she knew she might never see him again.

"Ryan," she paused to gain her thoughts. "I want you to know, no matter what has happened or what you've done, God is real and cares about you."

It was impossible to quickly dismiss someone as genuinely kind as April. Ryan hadn't thought about God or church for a long time.

"Thanks," he said quietly. "But you have no idea. God could never take me back now."

Can I do something so bad God won't forgive me?

q *(questions)*

What parts of this story jump out to you? Why?

What factors led to Ryan's statement,
"God could never take me back"?

Have you ever been able to relate to Ryan? How?

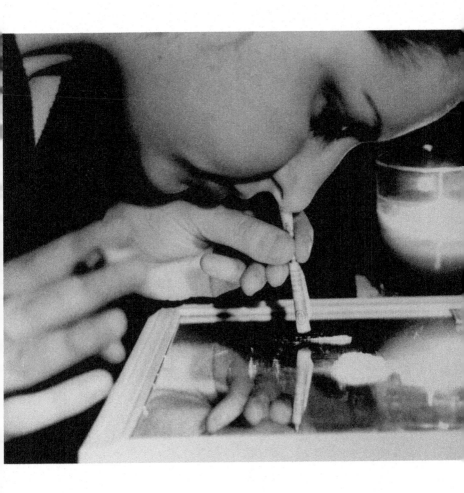

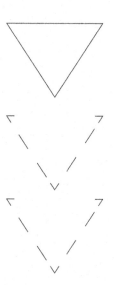

One-Verse Wonders

When looking for help in scripture, it often can be tempting to read one Bible verse and see if it gives you direction. Sometimes people jump to conclusions because of one verse. Ryan did this, and the results were not good. When reading the Bible, make sure you read the verses before and after the particular verse you are interested in. It helps to know the broader picture of why that verse is being written and to whom. Finally, almost every topic you find in the Bible can be found in more than one place. Ask someone you trust to help you understand what other voices across the span of scripture might add to the same topic.

Don't Sin Ever Again

Paul, who wrote a lot of the New Testament, is the kind of guy who probably never sinned, right? Well, Romans 7:14-25 is Paul's confession that sin often dominated his life, even after he started following Jesus. Paul talked about the "sinful nature" inside of him that acted against what God's Spirit wanted to do. He described the sinful nature and the Holy Spirit like a "war" inside of him.

> What are some things you wish you could stop doing, but you don't seem to be able to stop?

Sacrificing Lambs

In the Old Testament, people would kill animals as a sacrifice for the sins they committed. The "sacrificial lamb" was an animal given to God as worship (usually burned on an altar as an offering or way to apologize for the people's sins and make things right. Under the Old Testament understanding of God's law, this animal's death substituted for the person's own death.

Why Did Jesus Die?

Jesus is called "the lamb of God, who takes away the sin of the world" (John 1:29). Jesus' sacrifice is all that is needed to cover our sins. That does not mean you will never sin again. It does mean that Jesus died to forgive you for all the wrong you've done in your past, your present, and everything you will do wrong in the future, too. Jesus' death and resurrection ushered in the beginning of the new creation, and we are waiting for Jesus to come again and make all things new—including us! But between now and then, even in the midst of our ongoing spiritual growth, we still struggle with sin and its results.

What does our culture say the "worst" sins are? What have you heard Christians say?

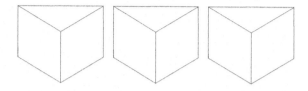

The Unforgivable Sin

There is one sin that Jesus refers to as being "unforgivable" in Mark 3:28-29. What is Jesus talking about?

How Do We Handle Mistakes?

When we make mistakes—even big ones—Jesus has given us a way to respond. 1 John 1:9 assures us, "If we confess our sins, he is faithful and just and will forgive us our sins and purify us from all unrighteousness." Confession, which just means telling the truth, is a way to be honest before God about the ways we have blown it.

(*scripture*)

We mentioned Paul earlier. He wasn't always called Paul. Saul was his original name, and he was a key Jewish religious leader after Jesus' death and resurrection. Saul hated that people were starting to believe in Jesus, and it caused him to respond violently. Saul was present when a man named Stephen told a group of religious leaders about Jesus. It didn't go very well for Stephen.

Read Acts 7:57–8:3:

At this they covered their ears and, yelling at the top of their voices, they all rushed at him, dragged him out of the city and began to stone him. Meanwhile, the witnesses laid their coats at the feet of a young man named Saul. While they were stoning him, Stephen prayed, "Lord Jesus, receive my spirit." Then he fell on his knees and cried out, "Lord, do not hold this sin against them." When he had said this, he fell asleep. And Saul approved of their killing him.

On that day a great persecution broke out against the church in Jerusalem, and all except the apostles were scattered throughout Judea and Samaria. Godly men buried Stephen and mourned deeply for him. But Saul began to destroy the church. Going from house to house, he dragged off both men and women and put them in prison.

– Acts 7:57–8:3

In ancient times, people would kill someone by throwing rocks at them until they died, which was called stoning. That's how Stephen died.

According to this passage, of what crime is Saul guilty?

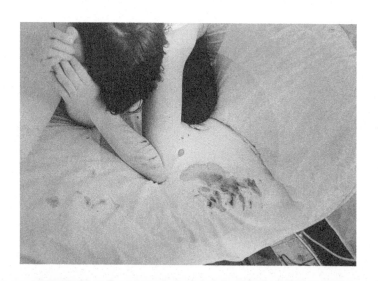

Saul's life was changed when he met Jesus

(that story is recorded in Acts 9). He eventually changed his name to Paul and was the driving force behind the spread of Christianity all across the ancient world. How did Paul view his terrible past?

Read what Paul wrote later in a letter:

— — — — —

> *Here is a trustworthy saying that deserves full acceptance: Christ Jesus came into the world to save sinners—of whom I am the worst. But for that very reason I was shown mercy so that in me, the worst of sinners, Christ Jesus might display his immense patience as an example for those who would believe in him and receive eternal life.*
>
> – 1 Timothy 1:15-16

What do you notice about what Paul says in this passage? What feelings does that stir in you?

Did Paul really believe he was forgiven for committing murder? What can we learn from his belief?

Is it possible that Jesus' power shown through his ministry, death, and resurrection is big enough to cover any mistake you could make?

(talk)

Pretend you are talking with some friends who give their opinions on this topic. Read their comments and, on a scale from 1-10 (where 1 is "totally disagree," and 10 is "totally agree"), rate how much you agree with each person's statement.

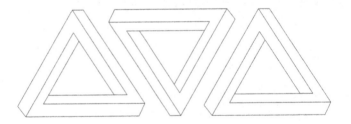

TYLER

I've heard God forgives me, but I don't believe it. Look at how so many people in churches are so judgmental and cruel to other people who have messed up. I can't believe God forgives when people in the church don't seem to do it themselves.

        1   2   3   4   5   6   7   8   9   10

SARAH

I'm so thankful God has forgiven me. I don't think I have anything really bad to forgive, but it's amazing that God forgives everything, even the little things.

        1   2   3   4   5   6   7   8   9   10

SEAN

As long as I keep trying my hardest to be good, I know God will forgive me. If you stop working at becoming a better person, you aren't really a Christian. It's clear to me that God forgives everything as long as you are making a good effort.

        1   2   3   4   5   6   7   8   9   10

AMY

If God forgives everything, I'm going to just keep doing all the fun stuff I feel like doing, even if it's supposedly a sin. Why shouldn't I? I know God will forgive me in the end if I ask for it.

        1   2   3   4   5   6   7   8   9   10

How would you respond next in this conversation if they asked you to share what you think about God's forgiveness?

What other questions do you have now about this topic?

Ideas / Notes

Session

4 | *Why do bad things happen to good people?*

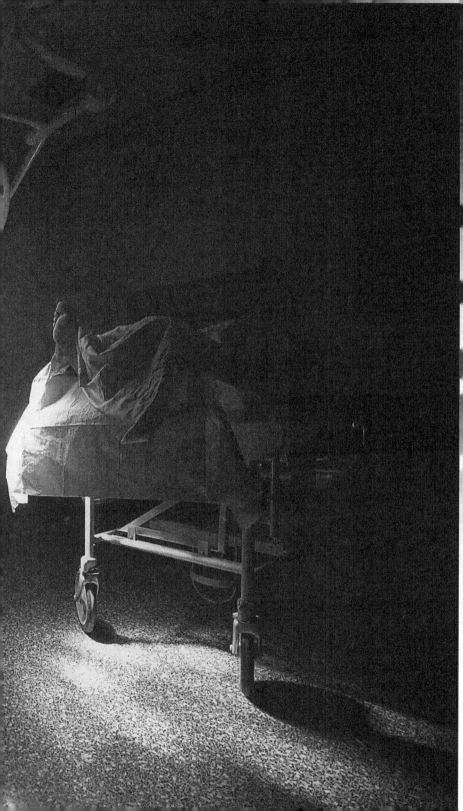

Carina will never forget her school's Science Fair Night.

She was a freshman, and her project predicted the year's first snow date based on the last 100 years of data. Carina loved the project and got a great grade, but her memory of the night was forever changed the next morning in her first period science class.

She was running late to school, had forgotten her phone, and rushed in just barely before the bell. Immediately, Carina noticed a few of the other kids were in tears. She also realized her good friend, Jenny, was absent.

"I'm guessing most of you have heard this, but this is a really tragic day." Mrs. Thompson's voice cracked a little on the last word. "Last night Jenny was killed in a car accident."

Carina felt like someone had punched her in the chest. She lost her breath and felt tears burst from her eyes. This news could not possibly be true, could it?

Jenny and her family had left Science Fair Night just like everyone else. They turned down Pine Avenue and saw a car coming at them in the distance. It was swerving all over the road out of control. Immediately, they knew the driver was drunk.

Jenny's dad pulled over onto the shoulder of the road as far as he could in order to get out of the way. They watched in horror as the drunk driver plunged off the opposite side of the road, redirected the car, and came back out of the ditch. The car flew across the road and slammed into the side of Jenny's car.

Jenny died on impact.

Her parents walked away unharmed physically, but they were emotionally tormented. Could they have done something different? Was there a way they could have saved Jenny? They would wonder about these questions for years, battling depression, self-doubt, and anger. Jenny was their only child.

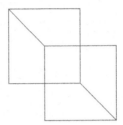

Meanwhile, Mrs. Thompson's science class was also devastated. Jenny's best friend Tanya could hardly speak. Tanya, Jenny, and Carina attended the same church together, and all their lives people had told them things like, "God loves you," and, "God is your shield of protection."

The class sat and cried together in an empty attempt at consolation. But Tanya and Carina couldn't escape one haunting question:It's time to learn a fancy new word. The question of why God permits evil to harm good people is not

How could God love us and let this happen?

q (questions)

Jenny's death was the result of someone else's huge mistake. How do you explain why God allows tragedies like this to happen?

What story in our community or your own life comes to mind when you read about this?

What are some of the things you hear people say following tragedies that kind of become cliché phrases? How do you feel when you hear these responses?

How could God love us and let bad things happen?

 *(notes)*

Theodicy

a new question. People have asked this question for centuries. It even has its own term: theodicy. A theodicy is an attempt to explain the relationship between our suffering and the nature of God.

Many "Theodicies"

People respond several ways when confronted with tragedy:

1. The existence of pain means God is real but isn't good and loving.

2. God isn't powerful enough to stop bad things from happening.

3. God doesn't care and isn't powerful—a combination of the first two.[1]

4. God allows suffering because we are given free will to choose to do good or bad.

5. God must not exist at all (this is called atheism).

6. Evil is a result of satanic and/or demonic powers, and our lives are caught up in a cosmic battle in the spiritual realm between evil and good.

7. Karma is the notion that you get what you deserve in this life based on your actions in a previous life (the belief in reincarnation accompanies this theory).

Do you or someone you know fit one of the responses above because of some hard things that have happened?

What other explanations have you heard for the problem of the coexistence of both a loving God and our human suffering?

What Sin Really Does

Much of human suffering can be understood more clearly from Genesis 3, the story of the first couple choosing together to disobey God. At the core of sin is humanity's rebellion against God. When those first human beings sinned (and when we sin), four key relationships were broken: our relationships with God, ourselves, each other, and the world around us.

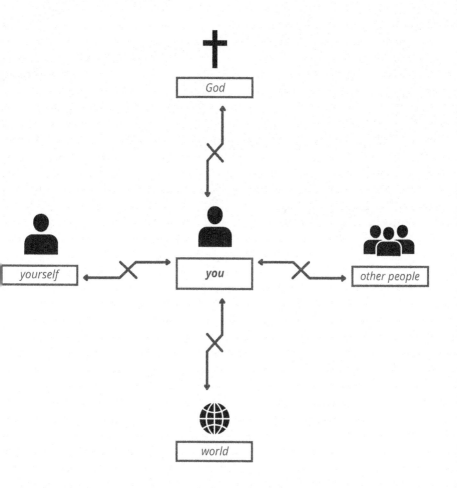

Why do bad things happen to good people?

S (scripture)

Read John 16:32-33:

A time is coming and in fact has come when you will be scattered, each to your own home. You will leave me all alone. Yet I am not alone, for my Father is with me. I have told you these things, so that in me you may have peace. In this world you will have trouble. But take heart! I have overcome the world.

– John 16:32-33

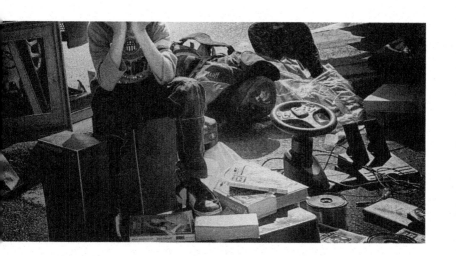

Why are these verses important to this discussion?

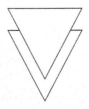

Now read Isaiah 53:3-6:

He was despised and rejected by mankind,
a man of suffering, and familiar with pain.
Like one from whom people hide their faces
he was despised, and we held him in low esteem.
Surely he took up our pain
and bore our suffering,
yet we considered him punished by God,
stricken by him, and afflicted.
But he was pierced for our transgressions,
he was crushed for our iniquities;
the punishment that brought us peace was on him,
and by his wounds we are healed.
We all, like sheep, have gone astray,
each of us has turned to our own way;
and the LORD has laid on him
the iniquity of us all.

– Isaiah 53:3-6

This Old Testament prophecy was fulfilled in Jesus. How does it feel to hear that Jesus was despised, rejected, a man of suffering, and familiar with pain?

Finally, read Revelation 21:4

"He will wipe every tear from their eyes. There will be no more death" or mourning or crying or pain, for the old order of things has passed away.

– Revelation 21:4

What is this verse referring to? How can there possibly be a day when God will eliminate all suffering?

Have you ever seen anything good eventually come out of something terrible? What was it?

 *(talk)*

Imagine you are with some friends who start talking about the question of why bad things happen to good people. Read their viewpoints and write one sentence in each space provided with a summary of how you think that person views both God and suffering.

SHAWNA

I hear Christians say stuff like, "God works out all things for good," and I want to scream. That sounds nice until you are the one suffering. When my parents got a divorce, someone told me it was all in God's plan. Can you believe how insensitive that is?

_____

CAL

I don't understand how God created a world with evil in it. If God created everything, doesn't that mean that somewhere in God, evil exists? I can't trust that kind of God.

_____

NATE

It bothers me when people question God. I had someone ask me
once how God could allow a tsunami to kill thousands of people,
and I told them to stop questioning God. You just have to trust
that God knows how to run things better than you do.

TRAYLON

We can't understand why God allows evil. It's a mystery. I have
a nightmare situation I'm walking through right now that I can't
even talk about. I hope it's true that God can use things like
that for good. I'm putting all my trust into that being true.

Any last thoughts or questions you want to
share on this topic?

Footnotes

1. See C.S. Lewis, *The Problem of Pain*, for a more detailed description of these positions. Lewis, who lost his wife to cancer, wrote about God's goodness in the face of suffering.

Ideas / Notes

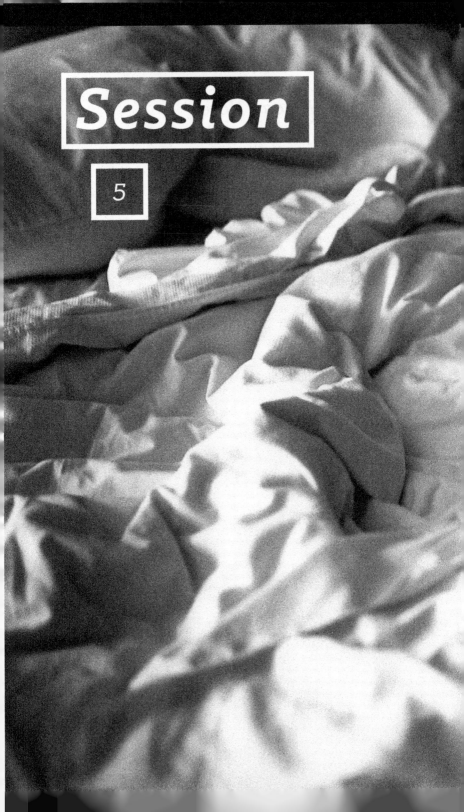

Session

5

Is sex outside marriage wrong?

Trevor's first clue was a text from his friend Walker

jonah's parents told me he's staying @ ur house tonight. can I come over & drop off the money I owe him?

"That's weird," Trevor thought. "Jonah isn't staying at my house tonight." He decided to text Jonah and see what was happening.

Hey – Walker thinks ur spending the night over here. What's up?

A few minutes later Jonah responded:

I'll tell u what's up later. if my parents call, tell them I'm at ur house using the bathroom then text me right away.

Trevor and Jonah were both juniors and had been friends for over 10 years. This was the first time Jonah had ever done anything

like this. What was he doing? Was he in trouble? Why was he hiding from his parents? Trevor decided to text Jonah's girlfriend, Ruthie, to see if she knew anything.

Do you know where Jonah is?

Ruthie didn't respond. Trevor found out the next day what had happened. Ruthie's parents had left town and Jonah stayed at her house.

"We did it," Jonah said with a grin. "Ruthie and I had sex last night."

Trevor tried not to look surprised. A couple of years earlier, both Trevor and Jonah had heard a talk at their church that motivated them to make a decision not to have sex unless they got married. *What happened?*

"We love each other," Jonah said. "We finally woke up and figured out that there was no reason to hold back any longer. Why should we wait? What could be wrong about something so natural?"

q *(questions)*

What do you think of Jonah and Ruthie's decisions? Why?

What do you think of Jonah's last comment in the story—"What could be wrong about something so natural?"

What do you think are the pros and cons of having sex outside of marriage?

n *(notes)*

Sex Is God's Idea

Don't let anyone tell you sex is wrong. The truth is that sex is God's idea and it is good. In the very beginning God made Adam and Eve and told them (commanded them, actually) to populate the earth—that meant having sex (see Genesis 1:28).

Have you ever talked to God about your relationships with the opposite sex?
Why or why not?

Sexual Immorality

While there is no verse that specifically says, "Don't have sex before marriage," Paul consistently speaks against all forms of "sexual immorality" (see Ephesians 5:3, 1 Corinthians 6:18, and 1 Thessalonians 4:3-5). New Testament scholars typically affirm that this term "sexual immorality" includes sex outside of marriage.

Polygamy

Polygamy is a word that means "having more than one spouse." One argument for waiting for marriage to have sex is that God intended sex to be between just two people. If that is truly God's intention, why is the Old Testament filled with men like Jacob, Solomon, and David who had more than one wife? In fact, by the biblical account, Solomon seems to have had sex with over 1,000 women![1]

One Spouse

While the Old Testament took place during an era when men would marry multiple women, that doesn't mean it was God's intention, even though it may have been a cultural norm. Paul (who wrote much of the New Testament) teaches in his writings that marriage is intended to be between just two people in verses like 1 Corinthians 7:1-5 and 1 Timothy 3:2. There are some ancient practices (like polygamy) that the writers of the New Testament condemned.

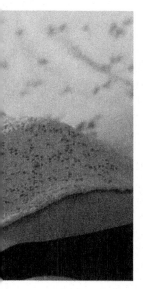

Covenant

The main way marriage is spoken of in scripture is a covenant relationship. A covenant is more than a promise; it's a deep commitment to be kept until one or both parties die. In fact, both the Old and New Testaments often use marriage as a metaphor to describe our relationship with God. See Isaiah 62:5 and Revelation 19:7-9 for two examples. In this covenant, God promises to be faithful to his vows forever.

(*scripture*)

Read Jesus' words in Matthew 19:4-5:

> "Haven't you read," he replied, "that at the beginning the Creator 'made them male and female,' and said, 'For this reason a man will leave his father and mother and be united to his wife, and the two will become one flesh?'"
>
> – *Matthew 19:4-5*

What do you notice about Jesus' words on marriage?

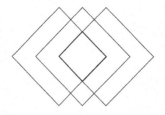

Now read 1 Corinthians 6:18-20:

Flee from sexual immorality. All other sins a person commits are outside the body, but whoever sins sexually, sins against their own body. Do you not know that your bodies are temples of the Holy Spirit, who is in you, whom you have received from God? You are not your own; you were bought at a price. Therefore honor God with your bodies.

– 1 Corinthians 6:18-20

What does it mean that your body is a "temple of the Holy Spirit"?

If my body is God's temple, how far is too far?

Read 1 Corinthians 10:13:

No temptation has overtaken you except what is common to mankind. And God is faithful; he will not let you be tempted beyond what you can bear. But when you are tempted, he will also provide a way out so that you can endure it.

– 1 Corinthians 10:13

Why is this verse important to this particular discussion?

What happens if I mess up, or if I messed up (even a lot) already?

 (*talk*)

Pretend you are with some friends who start talking about sex. Read their viewpoints and follow the instructions below.

ELLA

Not only is sex before marriage wrong, but we shouldn't come close to tempting ourselves. My first kiss is going to be with my husband during our wedding. If we're really going to be pure, like the Bible says, we shouldn't do anything physical until we get married.

PABLO

As long as you're safe about sex, why would God stop us from enjoying it? It's an old-fashioned idea that sex outside of marriage is wrong. The world has progressed and so should Christians.

ABBY

I think you should only have sex with one person, but it's OK if that's before marriage. If you love each other and you know you are going to get married, you should probably have sex with that person to see if you are a true match. It would be terrible to get married and find out you're not very compatible sexually.

JACK

I'm going to get married before I have sex. People think I'm crazy, but I want to share that only with my wife and no one else. It's a struggle to wait, though. My girlfriend and I are tempted all the time.

Which of the above voices most closely represents how most people you know would look at the issue of sex outside of marriage?

Who do you think you'd want to talk with more about their view? What would you want to say to them?

Based on what we've discussed today, what personal decisions would you like to make about sex?

What other questions do you have about this topic?

Footnotes

1. 1 Kings 11:1-3. Note that if you read on in chapter 11, things did not go well for Solomon because of this.

Ideas / Notes

Session

6

Why is it so awkward to talk about Jesus with my friends?

Kali first started drinking alcohol her sophomore year

when her older sister began giving her cases of beer to share with her friends. Her life became one party story after another. But she always felt like there was something more to live for—something less empty.

That emptiness changed the summer before her senior year. Manny, her good friend from the guys' lacrosse team, invited Kali to his house and said, "I need to talk to you about something important to me."

Kali could tell Manny was suddenly very nervous. Manny started sharing about his faith in Jesus, and he even pulled out a Bible and read a couple of verses. At first it was totally awkward, but then for some reason it began to click for Kali.

"Yeah," Kali said. "My life's a mess. I want to believe in God, and I don't totally understand it, but I want to follow Jesus." They prayed together for God to help Kali and for Jesus to become her Lord.

Kali's life changed a lot. She started

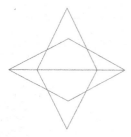

growing in her faith and trusting God. She even started going to a Christian group that met in people's homes to talk about Jesus with other high school students. At one of those meetings, one of the older college student leaders shared how he tried to twist every interaction he had with someone who wasn't a Christian into a "spiritual" conversation. Whether they were talking about football or finals, he figured out how to talk about how much people need Jesus. Maybe it was just his cool beard and easy smile, but he made it seem really natural.

'Jesus wants you to tell your friends about God," the leader said. "Pray right now for who the Holy Spirit wants you to share with. Then come back next week and we'll share some awesome stories about what happened."

Kali was terrified. She thought, *God really wants me to do this? What if I get rejected?*

After praying, Kali decided to talk to Lizi. Lizi was one of her "party" friends, and Kali considered Lizi one of her closest friends. Kali passed her in the hall at school and summoned up her courage to ask Lizi to eat lunch with her so they could have a serious talk.

At lunch, Kali pivoted the conversation from the math test they had just taken to talking about why Lizi needed to follow Jesus because she needed to be saved from her sin, just like the college leader had described. When Kali finished, she looked at Lizi awkwardly, waiting for her response.

"Are you serious?" Lizi said. "This is what you wanted to talk about?"

"Yeah," Kali said. "It's important to me, and I don't want you to be separated from God anymore." She had heard one of the leaders at the group use that phrase.

"I seriously think you must be joking," Lizi said, anger flashing in her eyes. "Ever since you started this 'God thing,' you've changed. And I don't like how you've changed. You're becoming such a freak."

Lizi picked up her food and left Kali sitting alone. She felt embarrassed and confused, and she wondered what she had done wrong.

(questions)

What did you notice in this story?

Has anyone ever tried to share their religious beliefs with you? What happened?

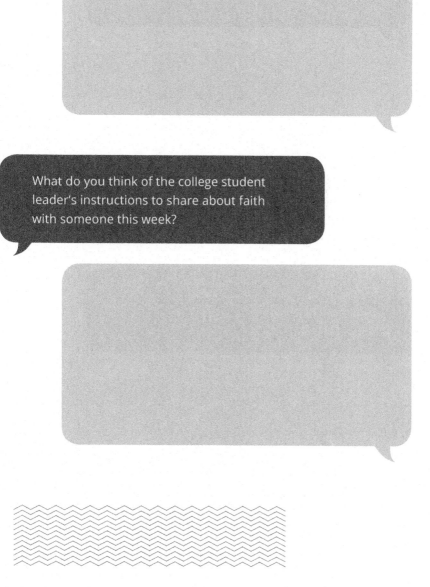

What do you think of the college student leader's instructions to share about faith with someone this week?

Why do you think Kali responded to her
conversation with Manny positively, while Lizi
just got angry?

Why would anyone feel the need to share
their faith with someone else? Why not just
keep it private?

(notes)

The Great Commission

Jesus himself is the source of our call to share our faith in God with others. Jesus' last words in Matthew's gospel are often called "The Great Commission" (though Jesus himself didn't use that language). Commission is a fancy word meaning an official task that has been given to someone; at its core this passage is about Jesus sending out his followers to share his message. Check out Matthew 28:18-20:

Then Jesus came to them and said, "All authority in heaven and on earth has been given to me. There-fore go and make disciples of all nations, baptizing them in the name of the Father and of the Son and of the Holy Spirit, and teaching them to obey every-thing I have commanded you. And surely I am with you always, to the very end of the age."

– Matthew 28:18-20

Do you think this passage specifically says that Jesus wants us to share our faith? Why or why not?

The original tone of Jesus' words indicated something ongoing, so we might also translate this, "as you are going ...." That can mean as you're going to school, to band practice, or to the other things that are part of your normal life, as much as it might mean going around the world.

Evangelism

You've probably heard this word before, but what does it mean? The original Greek word for evangelist meant something like "one who brings a good message." Sharing the message of Jesus, or being an evangelist, is listed as one of the ways God equips people to serve him, also known as a "spiritual gift" (Ephesians 4:11).

> What if I don't think I have the gift of evangelism? Does that mean I don't have to tell others about God?

Gentleness and Respect

The Bible gives us clues on how we should share our faith. The author of 1 Peter is writing to encourage Christians who are hated because of their faith. In the midst of that context, 1 Peter 3:15 says, "But in your hearts revere Christ as Lord. Always be prepared to give an answer to everyone who asks you to give the reason for the hope that you have. But do this with gentleness and respect." Even in the face of being disliked for our faith in God, Peter invites us to share our faith with respect for the other person.

> What ideas does this give you about how you could talk about faith with someone else?

Dialogue vs. Monologue

Another clue about sharing faith is found in Acts 17:16-34. Paul was in the city of Athens where the people believed in many different gods. Paul modeled the type of conversations we can have today by genuinely listening to others. He even complimented them for being "religious" and invited them to notice how their beliefs and openness to spirituality pointed toward Jesus.

If I'm respectful in telling someone about Jesus and they still reject me, did I do something wrong?

Announcing the Kingdom

The writers of the New Testament Gospels talked about Jesus' mission as announcing the kingdom—or reign—of God. This is the essence of the "good news"—that God is breaking through to us and has, through Jesus, begun making all things new. We live in the in-between time when the reign of Jesus as Lord has begun, but it isn't yet complete. During this season, we are invited to join in God's mission to make all things new. Sharing the gospel—through words, service, acts of compassion, and our very lives—is participating in the in-breaking Kingdom of God.[1]

(*scripture*)

You've heard it said plenty of times that actions speak louder than words. Words certainly matter, but the way we live reveals our real beliefs, convictions, and values. One of the reasons some people avoid Christians is a perception that believers are hypocritical and judgmental. On the flip side, sometimes people come to know Jesus through discovering a community that loves one another deeply and serves the community and the poor faithfully. As we develop a community that is loving and hospitable, we are sharing Jesus with others by what we do. Here's Jesus' take on this:

A new command I give you: Love one another. As I have loved you, so you must love one another. By this everyone will know that you are my disciples, if you love one another. ...

As the Father has loved me, so have I loved you. Now remain in my love. If you keep my commands, you will remain in my love, just as I have kept my Father's commands and remain in his love. I have told you this so that my joy may be in you and that your joy may be complete. My command is this: Love each other as I have loved you. Greater love has no one than this: to lay down one's life for one's friends. You are my friends if you do what I command. I no longer call you servants, because a servant does not know his master's business. Instead, I have called you friends, for everything that I learned from my Father I have made known to you.

—John 13:34-35; 15:9-15

What surprises you about what Jesus says here?

How does what we read earlier about sharing about Jesus with gentleness and respect in 1 Peter 3:15 relate to Jesus' teachings in John?

How do you see believers living out these commands today? How can that be a way to share our faith with others?

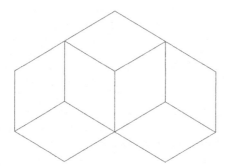

Has trusting and following Jesus impacted your life in a way that you'd want to tell someone else about? How? What would you want to share?

 *(talk)*

Pretend you are with some friends who give their opinions on this topic. Read their comments and answer the questions below.

NATALIE

I think it's offensive when people share their faith. It doesn't matter if you're Christian, Muslim, Jewish, or whatever. Just keep your belief in God to yourself and everyone will be happy.

TODD

Waiting until you have a good relationship with someone before you share Jesus with them is just an excuse to put off what you know you should be doing. God is looking for people with the courage to be bold about Jesus and not be so scared all the time.

PHOEBE

I think the best way to share Jesus with someone is just to invite them to church. I get scared about sharing my faith, and the pastor at my church is so great at explaining it all. Why take the chance of messing it up?

TYLER

I hate those guys who preach in public places. They just
make people mad and not want to follow God even more. You
should know someone really well before you share about
Jesus. No one ever follows God because they've
been screamed at.

What person above do you most
relate to? Why?

Who do you least relate to? Why?

How do you want today's discussion to impact
the way you interact with your friends?

Footnotes

1. For a deeper exploration of these ideas, see N.T. Wright, *Surprised by Hope: Rethinking Heaven, the Resurrection, and the Mission of the Church* (New York: Harper Collins, 2008), in particular pp 207ff.

Ideas / Notes

10 Tips for reading your Bible

Hopefully this study has left you hungry to learn and grow more in your faith in God. One way to do that is by reading your Bible. Like anything worth doing, it takes some practice and time to know how to read it well. Here are a few tips on how you can get started or perhaps make your attempts at reading the Bible more meaningful.

Pray for the Spirit to Help You

You will not be able to understand the Bible well without God's help. Pray for the Holy Spirit to guide you when you read. Jesus told his followers, "When the Spirit of truth comes, he will guide you into all truth ..." (John 16:13). Take Jesus up on this promise and invite God to lead you. Ask God to give you a heart that is open to being changed.

Formation vs. Information

2

To read the Bible and grow from it, you need to learn a different way to read. In school, you usually read for "information." Reading for school often means you need to read as much as you can, as fast as you can. Why? Two words: FINAL EXAM.

But reading the Bible is more about "formation" than information. God is using the Bible to shape or form you into a new person. That doesn't happen by reading as fast as you can and trying to memorize facts. With the Bible, it's often just the opposite. Read the Bible slowly. Pray as you go. Stop and ask questions. There is no pressure to "get through it." *If you are just trying to get through the Bible, the Bible won't get through to you.*

No Shame

High school is often the first time people start to feel shame that they don't know much about the Bible. Don't fall into the trap of thinking everyone knows how to read the Bible except you. Many adults, probably even those who go to your church, don't know how to read it well.

Sometimes high schoolers feel like they are so "far behind" when it comes to Bible knowledge that they don't even try. Don't be afraid to be honest about what you do and don't understand about the Bible, and ask for help from a trusted leader (see #7 below).

4 | Get a Readable Bible

Did you know there are all kinds of Bible translations out there? Make sure your Bible has words that are easily understandable. The *King James Version* may not be your best choice, because it was translated in a language that was popular centuries ago. Some translations that are easier for students to read include the *New International Version (NIV), Common English Bible (CEB), New Revised Standard Version (NRSV), or the New Living Translation (NLT)*. Another version of the Bible called *The Message* utilizes modern phrases and expressions to communicate in today's language as much as possible, and it pulls out the verse numbers so the passages read more like a novel. Most of the excerpts in this study have been from the *NIV* translation. You might also want to look for a Bible that has extra notes for context, sometimes called a "Study Bible." Some of these are written especially for teenagers.

5

Don't Start at Start

Jim remembers getting his first Bible, opening it, and starting to read it just like every book he'd ever read; from the beginning to the end. He made it to Exodus before he quit. If you've never read the Bible before, *you may not want to start in Genesis*. Read one of the gospels first (Matthew, Mark, Luke, or John). Those books tell Jesus' story and are a great place to get started. Then go back and get a sense for the bigger story from Creation to New Creation (Genesis to Revelation).

6

Read the Notes Before the Book

A good Bible will often include notes that introduce each book. It is good to read those notes before you dive in. Bibles with a good introduction will help you understand the context of what you are reading. Context is important because it tells you wh is writing to whom and why they are writing.

7

Bible Reading is a "Team Sport"

When you begin reading the Bible, you will be confused at times. That is okay. Read with someone else who knows the Bible more than you do. Find a pastor at your church, another Christian group leader, a parent, or a friend who knows the Bible and can help you. Don't struggle through the Bible on your own!

8

Use Your Imagination

The Bible tells some of the greatest stories you'll ever read. It also does not always elaborate on important elements of those stories. When you read stories in the Bible, stop and ask questions like, "What was the person thinking and feeling? What would it have been like to be there?" Use your imagination when you read the Bible.

It's About God

The Bible is not a "nice road map" with good tips on how to live. The Bible is a collection of stories, poems, songs, and letters that work together to tell one big story about God and about us. There are great thoughts about living your life, but the goal of the Bible is to reveal God and to draw you into a relationship with God. Get to know God as you read it.

Stick With It!

Many people start the Bible, get confused, and quit. Don't let that be you. If you are confused, remember that you're not alone. Reading the Bible is much like learning to play an instrument or a new sport. The more you practice reading it, the more natural it will become. Don't give up.

Insider Tips

⊗ There are two major sections of the Bible: The Old and New Testaments. The Old Testament tells the story of creation, of the journeys of God's people, and of their anticipation of the coming of Jesus. It also includes books like the Psalms, which capture poetry and songs that span the breadth of human emotion and response to God. The New Testament tells the story of Jesus on earth and what his life, death and resurrection mean. It goes on to share about the earliest churches and some of their letters to one another about living out the way of Jesus together. It closes with visions of Jesus returning to make all things new, and a promise that he will bring those visions to reality some day.

⊗ The Bible is broken into chapters and verses. John 3:16 refers to a verse in the gospel of John, chapter 3, verse 16. The little numbers you find in the midst of the paragraphs and sentences are verse numbers and make things easier to find. Many Bibles include footnotes that refer you to other passages where you find a similar verse, idea, or an exact quote that is repeated by another author. Sometimes that can help you piece together the different parts of the story.

⊗ The Gospels are the four books that start the New Testament (Matthew, Mark, Luke, and John) and tell the story of Jesus. The word *gospel* means "good news."

Photos

Introduction

Laughing Buddha by Flickr user Swaminathan.
Stay in the Moment by Flickr user by Flickr user Lauren Rushing
Silence by Flickr user Rebecca Barray.
Echo Lake, California by Flickr user Stanislav Sedov.
Deserted by Flickr user Jay Parker.
Time to Get Lost by Flickr user Mateus Lucena.

Session 1

Just because we can't see over the mountain, doesn't mean that there's nothing behind it by Flickr user Ansel Edwards.
Untitled by Flickr user Jorge Gonzalez.
The Kiss by Flickr user Thomas Leuthard.
Seeing Stars... by Flickr user n.a.t.u.r.e.
Echo Room by Flickr user Lauren Rushing.
M. by Flickr user Liliana.
Building Safer Structures by Flickr user U.S. Geological Survey.
Zoriah by Flickr user Zoriah.
Fire y Flickr user Stephen Salomons.

Session 2

Death in Paris by Flickr user Hans Van Den Berg.
Exit by Flickr user W3155Y.
Grandmother by Flickr user Monica Antonelli.
Disused Factory by Flickr user Philippe Leroyer.
Goodbye Grandma Fanny by Flickr user Brian Wolfe.
Museum National d'Histoire Naturelle by Flickr user Philippe Leroyer.
Demonstration against the Notre Dame des Landes airport by Flickr user Philippe Leroyer.
One Crow Left of a Murder by Flickr user Mark Sebastian.
Doing bad things with body parts behind the shower curtain by Flickr user Socar Myles.
Sin techo / Homeless by Flickr user Hernán Piñera.
Barren Land by Flickr user Amr Tahtawi.

Session 3

Untitled by Flickr user Lauren Rushing
Weed by Flickr user Frank.
Untitled by Flickr user Gemma Bou.
And so do cars... by Flickr user Jamie Gerig.

Relaxing After Work by Flickr user andronicusmax.
Silence by Flickr user Rebecca Barray.
Drinking buddies by Flickr user Gato-gato-gato.
Tonight by Flickr user 30dagarmedanalhus
Drugs by Flickr user Daniel Foster.

Session 4

Belvoir Park hospital Belfast by Flickr user Stefan Ray.
Untitled by Flickr user Lauren Rushing.
Move it Driver by Flickr user Mike Babiarz.
Car wreck in front of Manhattan bridge by Flickr user Adrian8_8.
Teenager say yes by Flickr user Mehmet Nevzat Erdoğan.
Untitled by Flickr user Sean Donohue.
This morning the lowness has won by Flickr user Kelsi Barr.
Childhood Denied by Flickr user Sergio Pani.
Silhouette by Flickr user Flood G.

Session 5

Scene of the Crime by Flickr user Ben Disinger.
Sex by Flickr user Rupert Ganzer.
Untitled by Flickr user Lindsay Stanford.
Love by Flickr user Hans Van Den Berg.
29/52 by Flickr user Lauren Rushing.
Midday / It's cold out there by Flickr user Malloreigh.
Untitled by Flickr user Silvia Sala.
Young Love by Flickr user Syxrious Sergio.
Sunrise Contemplations by Flickr user Jesi.
Hey guys, this is Riley. He's perfect by Flickr user Lauren Rushing.

Session 6

Have, have not by Flickr user Khairul Nizam.
Night Drink by Flickr user Diego Sevilla Ruiz.
Memories by Flickr user Tippi T.
Back to School by Flickr user Nick Kenrick.
Venice Beach California by Flickr user Patrick Merritt.
Summer by Flickr user Basher Tome.
Sun and Sea – Nothing Better by Flickr user Jesi.
Locked in his world by Flickr user Hernán Piñera.
And the time stood still by Flickr user Johanna Herbst.
Afternoon Drinking Games by Flickr user Thomas Hawk.

CPSIA information can be obtained
at www.ICGtesting.com
Printed in the USA
BVOW03s1536080217
475633BV00008B/90/P

9 780991 488032